the SCIENCE *library*

ANIMAL LIFE

Steve Parker

Consultants: Chris Pellant and Helen Pellant

Miles Kelly
PUBLISHING

First published in 2004 by Miles Kelly Publishing Ltd
Bardfield Centre Great Bardfield Essex CM7 4SL

Copyright © 2004 Miles Kelly Publishing Ltd

This edition printed in 2008

2 4 6 8 10 9 7 5 3

British Library Cataloguing-in-Publication Data
A catalogue record for this book is available from the British Library

Editorial Director Belinda Gallagher
Art Director Jo Brewer
Editor Jenni Rainford
Editorial Assistant Chloe Schroeter
Cover Design Simon Lee
Design Concept Debbie Meekcoms
Design Stonecastle Graphics
Consultant Chris Pellant and Helen Pellant
Indexer Hilary Bird
Reprographics Stephan Davis, Ian Paulyn
Production Manager Elizabeth Brunwin

ISBN 978-1-84236-989-0

Printed in China

www.mileskelly.net
info@mileskelly.net

www.factsforprojects.com

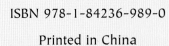

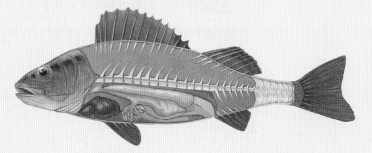

Contents

How to use this book

ANIMAL LIFE is packed with information, colour photos, diagrams, illustrations and features to help you learn more about science. Do you know which animals migrate to warmer countries or how meerkats warn each other of danger? Did you know the cuttlefish changes colour when it is angry or that there are fewer than 100 Javan rhinos alive today? Enter the fascinating world of science and learn about why things happen, where things come from and how things work. Find out how to use this book and start your journey of scientific discovery.

It's a fact
Key statistics and extra facts on each subject provide additional information.

Main text
Each page begins with an introduction to the different subject areas.

The grid
The pages have a background grid. Pictures and captions sit on the grid and have unique co-ordinates. By using the grid references, you can move from page to page and find out more about related topics.

Main image
Each topic is clearly illustrated. Some images are labelled, providing further information.

30

Breeding

BREEDING OR reproduction – making more of the same kind – is essential for all living things. Animals use many different methods. Some small and simple creatures, such as tiny tree-shaped hydras in ponds, simply grow offspring as 'stalks' on their own bodies. This is asexual (one-parent) reproduction. But most animals reproduce sexually, when a male and female mate. The male's sperm join with – fertilize – the female's eggs. The majority of creatures, from worms to birds, lay eggs. Only mammals and a few reptiles, fish and invertebrates, give birth to babies.

IT'S A FACT
• The female ling (a fish) produces over 20 million almost microscopic eggs.
• The female kiwi (a bird) lays just one egg each year, one-quarter of her size.

● **Wrong offspring**
The cuckoo is a 'reproductive parasite'. The female cuckoo replaces an egg in another bird's nest with her own egg, then flies away. The host bird looks after the new egg and chick, which pushes out the other chicks after it hatches.

Read further › nesting
pg22 (r3)

▲ These flycatchers are the ho... of this cuckoo chick, which m... eventually grow bigger than ...

▶ A baby elephant will stay with its mother for up to two years.

● **Parental care**
Larger mammals, such as elephants and apes, usually produce just one offspring and care for it over several years. Among a herd of elephants, other female elephants (cows) help to bring up the young and the 'family' members remain close throughout their lives. But smaller mammals, such as rats, may have ten or more babies that grow quickly and are independent in a couple of weeks.

Read further › apes
pg23 (p22)

The ostrich lays the world's biggest egg, 16 cm long and 14 cm deep

1 2 3 4 5 6 7 8 9 10 11 12 13 14 15 16

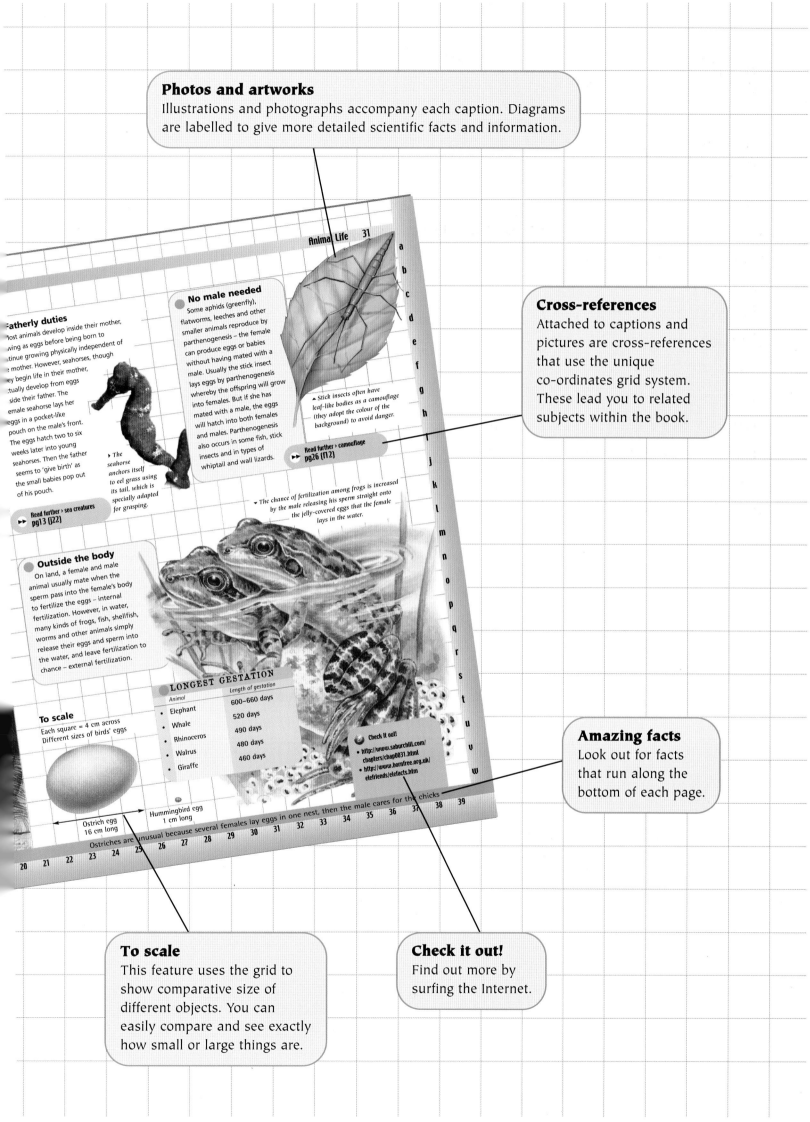

Photos and artworks
Illustrations and photographs accompany each caption. Diagrams are labelled to give more detailed scientific facts and information.

Cross-references
Attached to captions and pictures are cross-references that use the unique co-ordinates grid system. These lead you to related subjects within the book.

Amazing facts
Look out for facts that run along the bottom of each page.

To scale
This feature uses the grid to show comparative size of different objects. You can easily compare and see exactly how small or large things are.

Check it out!
Find out more by surfing the Internet.

The sample page shown:

Fatherly duties
Most animals develop inside their mother, growing as eggs before being born to continue growing physically independent of the mother. However, seahorses, though they begin life in their mother, actually develop from eggs inside their father. The female seahorse lays her eggs in a pocket-like pouch on the male's front. The eggs hatch two to six weeks later into young seahorses. Then the father seems to 'give birth' as the small babies pop out of his pouch.

▶ The seahorse anchors itself to eel grass using its tail, which is specially adapted for grasping.

Read further › sea creatures
pg13 (j22)

No male needed
Some aphids (greenfly), flatworms, leeches and other smaller animals reproduce by parthenogenesis – the female can produce eggs or babies without having mated with a male. Usually the stick insect lays eggs by parthenogenesis whereby the offspring will grow into females. But if she has mated with a male, the eggs will hatch into both females and males. Parthenogenesis also occurs in some fish, stick insects and in types of whiptail and wall lizards.

▲ Stick insects often have leaf-like bodies as a camouflage (they adopt the colour of the background) to avoid danger.

Read further › camouflage
pg26 (f12)

Outside the body
On land, a female and male animal usually mate when the sperm pass into the female's body to fertilize the eggs – internal fertilization. However, in water, many kinds of frogs, fish, shellfish, worms and other animals simply release their eggs and sperm into the water, and leave fertilization to chance – external fertilization.

▲ The chance of fertilization among frogs is increased by the male releasing his sperm straight onto the jelly-covered eggs that the female lays in the water.

To scale
Each square = 4 cm across
Different sizes of birds' eggs

LONGEST GESTATION	
Animal	Length of gestation
Elephant	600–660 days
Whale	520 days
Rhinoceros	490 days
Walrus	480 days
Giraffe	460 days

Check it out!
• http://www.saburchill.com/chapters/chap0031.html
• http://www.bornfree.org.uk/elefriends/elefacts.htm

Ostrich egg
16 cm long

Hummingbird egg
1 cm long

Ostriches are unusual because several females lay eggs in one nest, then the male cares for the chicks

Land movers

MOVEMENT DEFINES what an animal is. In general, animals can move from place to place but plants do not. Creatures travel about to find food and shelter, and avoid predators. Different types of animals use different parts of their bodies for movement. Most land (terrestrial) animals, from tiny bugs and spiders to large reptiles and mammals, use their legs for moving. But monkeys *(see pg29 [e36])* and sloths also swing by their arms, snails slide on their undersides, and snakes use their whole bodies. All movement uses muscles. Vertebrates (animals with a backbone) have muscles attached to the bones in their body. When the muscles pull on their bones, animals are able to crawl, walk, fly or swim.

(see pg29 [e36])

IT'S A FACT

• Reptiles were the first creatures to live entirely on land, over 350 million years ago.

• Bears are one of the few animals to walk on the soles of their feet.

• The African fringe-toed lizard has to dance across the hot sand in the desert to keep its feet cool.

Speed saves

Fast movement is most important in open habitats such as grasslands, where antelopes, gazelles and zebras need to escape from predators such as cheetahs, lions and wild dogs. Long, slim legs can be used to gain great speed. The muscles that help these animals to run are mainly in the upper leg and body, leaving the lower leg and foot very light so it can be moved to and fro faster when running at great speed.

▲ *The cheetah is the fastest land mammal, able to reach speeds of more than 100 km/h, but it can only maintain this speed for less than a minute.*

Read further › predators pg12 [d2]; pg13 [e22]

 Check it out!

• http://www.saburchill.com/ chapters/chap0005.html

Despite weighing over 2 tonnes, a rhino can charge with a burst of speed that would beat a human sprinter in a 100 m dash

1 2 3 4 5 6 7 8 9 10 11 12 13 14 15 16 17 18 19

Moving through soil

Burrowing animals use various methods of movement. The mole uses its powerful front legs as shovels to clear the earth away as it moves forward. The worm is like a tube of muscle that contracts to make its body hard, rather like a water-filled balloon, as the worm pushes between soil grains. Mole rats have straight limbs with five thick toes with claws for digging the soil.

▶▶ **Read further › teeth** pg12 (n2)

◀ *Sloths in South American rainforests are so well camouflaged that they do not need to race away fast to escape from predators.*

▲ *Naked mole rats of East Africa have massive incisors (front teeth) to eat and dig with. They are not really naked but have sparse hairs covering their pink bodies.*

Moving in trees

Sloths and gibbons travel through trees in different ways. A gibbon's arms are twice as long as its legs, with hook-shaped hands to hang from branches. Its swinging motion is called brachiation. The sloth hangs with four limbs, moving one at a time, and is the slowest moving animal at just 300 m/h.

Muscle power

Muscles get shorter, or contract, pulling different body parts, allowing movement. In vertebrates – fish, amphibians, reptiles, birds and mammals – the muscles are joined to bones which form an endoskeleton inside the body. In insects and spiders (see pg13 [j35]) they are joined to the hard outer body casing – the exoskeleton.

▶▶ **Read further › inside the body** pg16 (f2; s2)

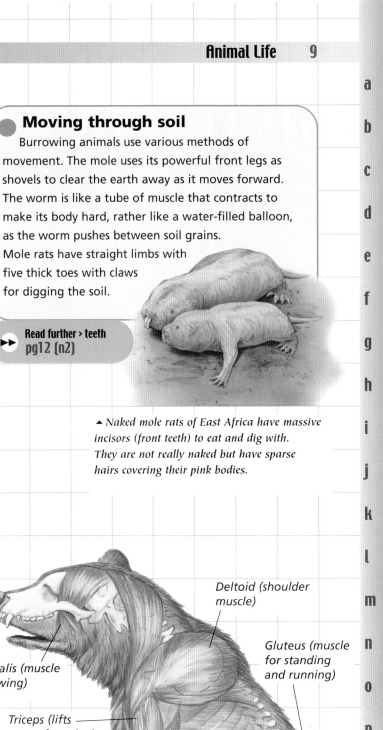

Deltoid (shoulder muscle)

Gluteus (muscle for standing and running)

Temporalis (muscle for chewing)

Triceps (lifts upper front leg)

Rectus (lifts upper rear leg)

Gastrocnemius (tilts back the rear paw)

SPRINT SPEEDS

Fastest land animals	Speed
• Cheetah	100 km/h
• Pronghorn antelope	90 km/h
• Springbok	80 km/h
• Ostrich	75 km/h
• Racehorse	70 km/h

▶ *Most mammals have a similar body structure, with muscles and limbs that work and move in the same way. This view of the inside of a bear shows some of the main muscles used for movement.*

The slowest land animals are snails, moving at only 15 cm a minute, 10,000 times slower than a cheetah can run

a b c d e f g h i j k l m n o p q r s t u v w

Soarers and swimmers

BOTH AIR and water are fluid – unlike solid ground they flow when you push them. So movement in air and water requires more muscle power. More than four-fifths of the body weight in a fish is muscle, compared to two-fifths of a land mammal. Fliers and swimmers both use broad pushing surfaces – wings through air, and fins, flippers and tails through water. These surfaces produce the propulsion (forward movement), while other body parts control steering and slowing down. In a bird, the main wing areas give propulsion, while the wingtips and tail provide control. In a fish, the tail is used for propulsion, and the side fins for control.

To scale
Each square = 6 m across
Some of the largest whales in the world

Blue whale 30 m

Fin whale 22 m

Sperm whale 20 m

Sei whale 16 m

Wing shapes
Hummingbirds and nectar-sipping bats flap their short, broad wings quickly, almost 100 times per second, to push air straight down so they can hover. In contrast, a wandering albatross can soar for hours on its long, slim wings without flapping once. Its 3.5 m wingspan glides the wind from the sea provides lift (upwards force).

▶▶ Read further › nectar eaters
pg15 [f22]

▲ *When a hummingbird hovers it tilts its head up and tail down to make its body vertical. Its wings flap in a curved figure of eight, and the whole wing twists at the joint with the body at each end of the stroke. This produces a more upward force, or lift, than simply flapping the wings to and fro.*

Check it out!

• http://www.saburchill.com/chapters/chap0012.html

Some tiny midges flap their wings more than 1000 times every second

◄ *One of the fastest fish, the bluefin tuna, can reach speeds of 70 km/h and migrate as far as 10,000 km across oceans.*

Kicking to swim

Many animals live both on land and in water, so they use their legs and feet to run and swim. The hippopotamus swallows plenty of air so that it can remain underwater for some time, then it can run along the riverbed. Otters, crocodiles *(see pg13 [u34])* and frogs have toes that are joined with flaps of skin, called webbing, to make a broad surface area for kick-swimming.

Swift swimmers

Water is very dense, so streamlining – a smooth body shape – enables fish, dolphins, seals and other sea creatures to move through it. Speedy fish such as marlin, tuna and wahoo have long, slim, tapering bodies that thin into a point. Thrust (the force to move forwards) comes from the tail, which is pulled from side to side by huge blocks of muscles along either side of the body.

Powerful rear legs kick off

Front legs cushion the landing

Webbed rear feet kick to swim and front legs steer through water

▲ *Many frogs move by leaping, which enables them to escape from predators quickly.*

Read further › dolphins
▶▶ **pg33 (d22)**

◄ *The 'flying squirrel' of North America can glide for more than 50 m, steering with its front legs, and slowing down or stopping by raising its tail.*

Gliders

Flying squirrels, possums, lemurs, fish, lizards, even frogs, do not really fly. The only animals that truly fly with power and control are bats *(see pg18 [h13])*, birds and insects. Others are gliders, using their broad surfaces like parachutes to swoop downwards. The best mammal glider, the colugo or flying lemur, can swoop for more than 200 m.

Read further › bats
▶▶ **pg18 (j12)**

CREATURE COMFORTS

• One of the most adaptable movers has no limbs at all. The golden tree snake can slither fast, swim well, burrow through loose soil, climb trees easily, and even launch itself from a branch and flatten its body to glide many metres.

• In habitats such as coral reefs, speed is not so important. Fish such as angelfish move their pectoral (front) fins to and fro like an oar, rather than by swishing their tails.

Up and down

Read further› shoals of fish
▶▶ **pg23 (d34)**

A dolphin's tail, called its flukes, looks similar to a fish's tail. A dolphin swims by arching its body up and down, not bending from side to side like a fish. Its flukes are not its 'legs' – they have no bones within them. However, its flippers, like a seal's flippers, are its 'arms', with hand and finger bones inside.

▸ *Dolphins have long streamlined bodies that are propelled through water by thrusts of their tails.*

A swan can flap its wings as slowly as once every second

Meat eaters

IT'S A FACT

• The biggest meat eater on Earth is not a lion or tiger but the sperm whale, which can weigh up to 50 tonnes.

• The smallest mammal carnivore is the pygmy shrew. Its head and body is as small as a child's thumb.

ANIMALS THAT eat mainly other animals are called carnivores. Some are active predators that hunt down prey, while others use stealth or ambush methods. Meat eaters range from killer whales and sharks in the sea, big cats and wild dogs on land, and eagles and hawks in the air, to much smaller but equally deadly shrews, bats, frogs, praying mantises, dragonflies, spiders and even sea anemones. Foods such as flesh, blood and eggs contain large amounts of nourishment and energy compared to plant foods. So carnivores spend less than one-tenth of the time eating than herbivores do. Animals such as monkeys that eat both plants and meat are called omnivores.

◀ Bears are the largest meat-eating land animals, feeding on meat such as fish and insects, as well as plants such as fruits, nuts and leaves. The sharp-ridged shape of their molar teeth has evolved to become more rounded for grinding plants and vegetation.

▼ This lion's skull shows a carnivore's teeth.

Incisors scrape meat from the bone

Canines stab and pierce flesh

Carnassials slide against each other to slice flesh

Hunting tools

Many carnivores have bodily weapons to jab into their prey, wound it and tear it apart to eat it. These include the strong, sharp, pointed teeth of sharks, alligators and mammals such as leopards, fang-like mouthparts in spiders, centipedes and predatory insects, sharp, hooked beaks of birds of prey, and the toe claws of birds and mammal hunters.

▶▶ Read further > leopards pg27 (k30)

◀ Leopards make large kills about every two days, taking their prey into trees away from scavengers such as hyaenas.

Check it out!

• http://www.saburchill.com/chapters/chap0014.html

• http://www.americazoo.com/goto/index/mammals/carnivora.htm

A shrew must eat every three hours or it can starve

1 2 3 4 5 6 7 8 9 10 11 12 13 14 15 16 17 18 19

◄ *With a wingspan of up to 2.3 m, the golden eagle swoops down to catch prey such as rabbits, grouse and other birds, seizing it with its sharp claws.*

Hunting methods

Techniques for catching prey vary greatly. Eagles and owls swoop down on to their prey silently and unnoticed from above. Wolves *(see pg23 [c25])* and wild dogs chase their prey over long distances. Cats creep near to victims and then rush or pounce on them. Some predators barely move. The shallow-water anglerfish lies camouflaged on the seabed attracting unwary victims with a fleshy blob of 'bait' on the end of its fin.

Read further › camouflage pg26 (g12); pg27 (b22)

Tied in strong silk

Many spiders spin webs and wait for their prey to get stuck in them. The spitting spider is more active. It stalks prey and then squirts a glue-like chemical from its fangs, which turns into sticky threads as it flies through the air and lands on the victim. The spider even shakes its head from side to side to make the threads zig-zag and glue down the prey. Then the spider uses its fangs for their normal purpose, to jab poison into its prey.

▼ *Spitting spiders, found mostly near human habitation, can only squirt their 'glue' up to 1 cm.*

Looks can deceive

Some animals that may not seem to be carnivores actually are. A starfish preys on shellfish stuck to the rocks, and can take a whole day to lever one open and digest its flesh. Sea anemones and jellyfish may look harmless but they actually eat fish, prawns and other victims.

Read further › seabed pg27 (b22)

Read further › crab spiders pg26 (s11)

◄ *Sea anemones wait for victims on the seabed and coral reefs, before trapping prey with their sticky, stinging tentacles.*

Feasting

Some hunters kill one large victim to last them a long time. A zebra or wildebeest can provide a crocodile with enough energy to last several months before its next meal. Other predators catch only tiny prey, but many of them. In one day a giant anteater consumes 20,000 ants and termites, and a blue whale *(see pg35 [g27])* can gulp in half a million child's toe-sized krill.

Read further › termites / ants pg22 (d2; o12)

CREATURE COMFORTS

• Mammals and birds of prey are warm-blooded, so they need to eat more food to provide the energy needed to heat their bodies, unlike cold-blooded animals.

• For this reason, a big cat must eat about ten times more food each year than a crocodile of similar body size.

▼ *Crocodiles glide underwater unnoticed before surging out of the water to catch their prey.*

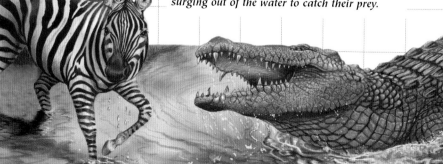

Some snakes can go for up to two years without eating between large meals

Plant eaters

MORE THAN three-quarters of all animals in the world are herbivores – plant eaters. In any habitat, there are always more herbivores than carnivores as the carnivores must feed on the plant eaters. Plant eaters range from elephants *(see pg30 [p14])* and hippopotamuses, to thousands of kinds of bugs, beetles, moths and caterpillars. However, few animals can eat all kinds of plants. They have adapted to eat certain plant parts. Some prefer soft, juicy leaves and flowers, while others chew tough roots or hard-cased nuts.

▲ Giraffes are 'browsers', chewing on vegetation regularly throughout the day. They use their comb-like canine teeth to strip leaves from branches and have a long tongue to gather leaves and shoots from high up in the trees.

● Living on leaves

Deer, most gazelles, giraffes and the black rhino are browsers, eating leaves from trees and shrubs. Zebras, wild cattle and the white rhino are grazers, consuming leaves or grasses from the ground. Most herbivore mammals have straight-edged front teeth for nibbling, and flat-topped cheek teeth, molars and pre-molars, for thorough chewing.

▶▶ Read further › teeth pg9 [b31]

● Tough to crack

Rodents such as rats, mice, beavers and squirrels use their long, continuously-growing front teeth (incisors) to crack the hardest seeds and nuts. Parrots *(see pg33 [b36])* and macaws do this using their beaks, while tortoises use their horn-rimmed, sharp-edged jaws.

▶ Because of their varied diet, rats spread all around the world, adapting to different conditions. A rat can cover up to 3 km in one night, foraging for food.

● CREATURE COMFORTS

• The only place on Earth where there are no plant eaters is at the bottom of the sea where there is no light for plants to grow.

• Most deep-sea animals are detritivores, consuming the decaying and rotting remains of dead creatures.

◀ *The yellow-bellied sapsucker of North and Central America feeds on sap from broadleaved trees such as poplar, birch and maple.*

Changing diet

Some plant eaters change their foods with the seasons. Pikas, which are small-eared relatives of rabbits, nibble buds and shoots in spring and grasses and herbs in summer. In autumn they store grass and leaves in piles near their burrow to eat during winter. Storing food to eat later in the year is called caching.

▼ *The North American pika chooses its food store for the winter depending on which plants decompose (rot) the slowest. This ensures that their food is not rotten before they can eat it all.*

Juice suckers

Sweet, sticky sap from plants and the sugary nectar made by flowers are packed with nutrients. Many plant eaters live only on this. The yellow-bellied sapsucker bird drills tiny holes through the trunk of a tree with its long, sharp beak and extracts the sap from inside the tree. Bugs such as aphids have needle-like mouths to jab into a stem and suck up the juice.

Read further › nectar
pg10 (n14)

Read further › winter
pg25 (n27)

▼ *This horse's skull shows a herbivore's teeth.*

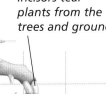

Incisors tear plants from the trees and ground

Row of large, broad-topped, crushing molars grind plants and vegetation

Gap (diastema) where canines used to be before herbivores adapted to plant-eating lifestyle

'Invisible' plants

Plants are the basic food for all animal life. On land, plants are easily seen. However, in the open ocean trillions of unseen microscopic plants called algae, that along with minute animals make up plankton, support animal life, too. They are eaten by whales and also tiny animals such as copepods, which become food for bigger sea creatures.

Read further › whales
pg35 (b22)

IT'S A FACT

• An elephant can consume up to 150 kg of food daily – the weight of two average-sized adult people.

• However, half of this food passes out the other end without being digested.

 Check it out!

• http://www.saburchill.com/chapters/chap0015.html

• http://www.nhm.org/mammals/page010.html

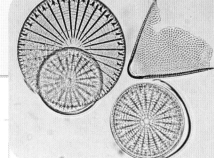

▶ *Microscopic diatoms and other algae provide food for tiny ocean plant eaters.*

The koala has one of the most restricted diets, limited to leaves from just a few eucalyptus trees

Digestion and respiration

EVERY ANIMAL needs a vital substance to stay alive – oxygen. It combines with food to provide energy for the huge variety of life processes inside the body. Oxygen makes up one-fifth of the air, and is also dissolved in water. Animals obtain it in different ways, but the parts which do so are always known as the respiratory system. Another main body need is nourishment – nutrients for growth, energy and day-to-day maintenance. In small and simple animals, nutrients can be taken in or absorbed through the body surface, especially in water where they are all around, in dissolved form. Larger animals have a specialized digestive system to obtain food and break it down into tiny parts or molecules, which can then be absorbed into the body.

Bones and joints

Brain

Gullet

Windpipe

Lungs

Kidney

Crop

Liver

Gizzard

Ovary

Heart

Intestine

Cloaca

▲ The lungs of the respiratory system and the heart from the circulatory system take up much of the front part of the body in the pigeon's chest. The digestive, excretory and reproductive systems fill the rear part of the body.

● The digestive system

The digestive tract is a passageway through the body from the mouth to the rear end. Different parts of it are designed for certain tasks. In a pigeon, the crop is like a storage bag for recently eaten food. The muscular gizzard grinds the food into a pulp and the intestine absorbs the various nutrients into the bloodstream. The kidneys are part of the excretory system that filter wastes from the blood to form a liquid – urine – that leaves the body through the cloaca to continually clear it of waste.

▶▶ Read further › urine scent pg21 (b22)

 Check it out!

• http://www.earthlife.net/birds/breath.html
• http://www.saburchill.com/chapters/chap0017.html

Gills for water

Gills are like 'inside out' lungs. They have the same branching, frilly structure but outside the body, in contact with water. Dissolved oxygen seeps from the water to blood flowing through the gills. Most water-dwellers have some type of gills, including fish, crabs and molluscs such as octopuses and sea-slugs.

Read further › fish senses
pg19 [c32]

▸ *Most fish have gills. This diagram shows part of a gill. Oxygen, from the water that flows over the gills, passes into the bloodstream of the amphibian.*

Primary gill filament (lamella or 'leaf')

Secondary gill filament (smaller lamella or 'leaf')

Low-oxygen water flows out through gill slit

Gill arch (stiff curve that holds out the gill filaments)

Oxygen in water passes into the blood flowing through gill filaments, turning it red

High-oxygen water flows in through mouth to gill chamber

Not all the same

The axolotl, a type of salamander, keeps its tadpole gills even when adult. The lungfish has gills but also pocket-like 'pouches' with blood-rich linings that branch off the gut. If its pool dries out, a lungfish swallows air into these pouches, which absorb the oxygen.

◂ *The axolotl has visible gills. If the gills become damaged, they quickly regrow.*

No special system

Small creatures such as flatworms have no special parts for respiration. Oxygen can pass straight through their thin skin. Their flattened shape means no part inside its body is more than a few millimetres away from the skin, so oxygen can easily seep this distance.

▴ *Many types of flatworm are parasitic – they live inside or attached to other creatures.*

Lungs for air

On land, vertebrates such as amphibians, reptiles, birds and mammals breathe air into lungs. Air tubes inside the lungs branch smaller and end in millions of microscopic 'bubbles', alveoli, which form a huge surface area and have plentiful blood in their linings. Oxygen from breathed-in air seeps into the blood and is spread around the body.

Read further › frogs
pg11 [c28]

Air spaces inside the lung

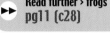

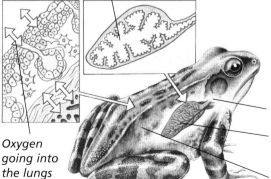

◂ *Frogs actually breathe through their skin as well as lungs.*

Windpipe

Lungs for breathing

Moist skin surface

Oxygen going into the lungs

CREATURE COMFORTS

• The bodies of mammals such as shrews work so fast to stay warm that they need more than 20 times more oxygen, compared to their body weight, than a large mammal such as a zebra.

• Warm-blooded animals need more oxygen than cold-blooded ones to 'burn' food to keep warm. A bird needs 15 to 20 times more oxygen than a lizard of the same size.

A whale breathes out or 'blows' 50 times harder than a human can blow

a b c d e f g h i j k l m n o p q r s t u v w

Animal senses

OVERALL, OUR own senses of sight, hearing, smell, taste and touch are good compared to many animals. But the senses of some animals are thousands of times better than ours, while others have senses that we do not have, such as being able to detect the natural magnetic force of the Earth. Each animal's senses are suited to its habitat and lifestyle, and especially the way it finds food and communicates. Night-time predators such as owls, cats and bats have big eyes to gather as much light as possible in the darkness. Creatures of the deepest seabed, where there is no light, have tiny eyes or none at all.

▸ The barn owl's ear openings are hidden under head feathers, but its hearing is very sensitive. One ear slightly higher than the other hears sounds coming up from the ground earlier than the other ear. These 'offset ears' allow amazingly accurate judging of the direction of a sound.

● IT'S A FACT

• The giant squid has eyes almost as large as soccer balls.

• An eagle or a hawk can see a rabbit moving from 5 km away.

◂ The bat moves its head from side to side as it flies. When it hears its high-pitched squeaks come back equally loud in both ears, it is directly facing the source of the echoes – its victim.

►► **Read further › bats**
pg11 (m22)

● Sight and sound

Owls are nocturnal – night-time – creatures so they need very acute hearing and large eyes to find their way at night. Bats have good sight, yet they cannot see in total darkness. They use their hearing in a system called echolocation to find their way, making high-pitched clicks and squeaks – pulses of ultrasound. When the noise hits an object, it bounces back as an echo and the bat is able to work out where the object is – even a tiny midge no larger than this full stop.

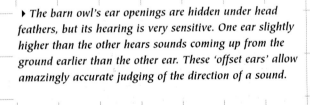

Dogs, bats and dolphins hear sounds 20 times more high-pitched than we can

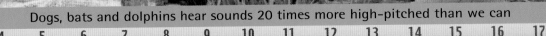

Smelling the air

Most animals have a better sense of smell than humans do. All animals that are hunted, from deer to mice, continually sniff the air for the scent of predators as well as for the smell of food. Smell works in water, too. Many fish have nostrils and can detect scents from many kilometres away.

▾ *The white-tailed deer is found between the regions of southern Canada and northern South America. It usually faces the wind when it rests and eats to detect any sign of danger.*

▶▶ Read further › scent
pg21 (j24)

▶▶ Read further › camouflage
pg26 (f2)

Taste sensors

In water, taste works on contact and also at a distance, rather like smell. A catfish is a 'living tongue' with taste buds over most of its body. It can also detect tiny electrical pulses passing through water. These come from the living bodies of other creatures nearby in the water, allowing the catfish to find prey that is hidden in the mud.

▴ *The catfish's front end bristles have sensors. It has tiny pits in the skin that detect electricity, smell detectors behind the nostrils, and touch and taste sensors all over its head, especially on its barbels or whiskers.*

Good vibrations

Like taste, touch works at a distance in water. Moving animals send out ripples that are detected by a fish's lateral line sense. This is a stripe along each side containing tubes or pits with very tiny hairs, which rock to and fro as ripples and water currents pass by.

Lateral line

CREATURE COMFORTS

• Insects have different eyes from other animals. They are made of many tiny parts, ommatidia, like a mosaic, each one detecting just a tiny part of a scene. A dragonfly has the biggest insect eye, with more than 30,000 ommatidia.

• Most insects hear with flexible flaps of skin, 'eardrums', which are actually found on the main body rather than on the head. Some grasshoppers have 'eardrums' on their knees.

▸ *The great barracuda has a strong lateral line sense and is a fast-moving predator, relying mainly on sight in the clear tropical waters.*

▶▶ Read further › movement in water
pg11 (d22)

🌐 **Check it out!**

• http://www.earthlife.net/birds/vision.html

Elephants and pigeons hear sounds 20 times lower-pitched than we can

a b c d e f g h i j k l m n o p q r s t u v w

Communication

COMMUNICATION MEANS passing on messages and information. People communicate by talking, making facial expressions or using body language such as waving. Animals use sound, sight and movement to communicate, as well as a range of methods including scent, taste, touch and the emitting of electrical signals. Some messages are understood only by their own kind, for example when a male frog croaks to attract a female of the same species at breeding time. Other messages can be understood by a wide variety of creatures – these are often about matters of life and death.

IT'S A FACT

• Lemurs have different calls to warn members of their troop whether danger is coming from above, along the ground, or is hidden in the undergrowth.

• Wolves and wild dogs smell each other's rear ends so that if they find droppings later they will know if a pack member left them – or a stranger.

▼ *The cobra's extended hood reveals a pattern that is on the rear of the hood, but shows through the stretched skin and thin, see-through scales.*

Warning signals

One sight-and-sound communication is widely understood in the animal world. This is rearing or puffing up to look bigger whilst making a hissing sound. This makes an animal seem bigger and fiercer, to warn off an attacker. A toad puffs up and makes a hissing sound, a cobra rears up, spreads its hood and hisses, and a cat's fur stands on end as it hisses.

▶▶ Read further › snakes and mimicry pg27 (c30)

▼ *While some meerkats gather food, others look out for predators, warning the group of danger by barking or shrieking loudly.*

Slap and thump

Sudden danger needs a short, sharp message to warn others in the group, and sound is often used. A meerkat shrieks shrilly, and many birds make a loud 'seep' or 'tic'. The first beaver to notice a predator nearby slaps its flat tail hard on the water's surface. A rabbit thumps the ground.

▶▶ Read further › defending territories pg28 (f2)

Check it out!

• http://www.enchantedlearning.com/subjects/rainforest/animals/Protection.shtml
• http://www.teachervision.fen.com/lesson-plans/lesson-142.html

Cuttlefish change colour with their mood – black means anger!

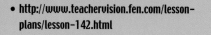

Leaving a message

Scent has an advantage over sights or sounds – it lasts after the sender has gone. Rhinos, hyaenas, sheep, foxes and many other animals spray strong-smelling urine or leave droppings around their territory. This shows the sex and age of the animal, and if it is ready for breeding.

◄ The male white rhinoceros marks his home range by spraying urine, leaving a scent. In order for a female to select a male rhino for breeding, the centre of his territory needs to be marked in this way to a distance of about 1 sq km.

Read further > marking territory
pg28 (f2); (n32)

A series of messages

Animals often give several messages before they take severe action against attackers. A skunk's black and white stripes are easily recognized when it lifts its tail as a warning to other animals to stay away. If an enemy ignores this, the skunk jumps from side to side, turns around, raises its tail and stands on its front paws before releasing a pungent spray from under its tail to put off the enemy.

Read further > sense of smell
pg19 (b22)

▼ The striped skunk, found across central North America, can eject its foul-smelling spray to a distance of up to 3 m away.

Where's the food?

Honeybees indicate to each other the site of a rich food source, such as nectar-laden flowers, by 'dancing'. The bee flies in a figure of eight and shakes its body. The angle of the '8' and the number of waggles convey the direction and distance of food from the nest.

Read further > nectar
pg10 (n14)

▸ In the bees' honeycomb dance, the angle between the straight crossover part of the '8' and the vertical, tells other bees the angle between the Sun and the direction of the food source.

CREATURE COMFORTS

• Yellow and black is one of the commonest colour combinations used as a warning, telling predators 'I taste horrible' or 'I am dangerous'. This pattern is used by various spiders, wasps, fish, butterflies, caterpillars, frogs and snakes.

• After an animal has had an unpleasant encounter with a yellow and black creature, the animal will avoid similar colours, which helps to protect all species with these colours.

A chimp that seems to us to be grinning widely, is really very afraid

Animal societies

IT'S A FACT

• The biggest animal societies are among termites. A large nest may contain over five million termites.

• Some marching columns of army ants in South America can number more than one million.

MOST ANIMALS, most of the time, live alone. They come together only to breed or raise a family. Some creatures gather in groups, in herds, flocks and shoals, often to use the same food source or for safety in numbers as they travel or rest. Only a few kinds of animals live closely together for long periods and interact with others of their kind. The most sociable animals are insects such as bees, ants and termites, a few types of fish and birds, and among mammals, types of wild dogs and many monkeys and apes.

▲ Male weaverbirds use their nests to attract a female with which to breed.

Bird village

Sociable weaverbirds make their nests out of stems, leaves and twigs. These individual nests are joined together, with as many as 300 forming one giant mass, usually in a large tree. The birds watch for danger together and gather to flap and peck at enemies. But they feed and raise their young separately.

▶▶ **Read further › danger warning**
pg20 (q12)

Chemical communication

In many insect societies, chemical substances called pheromones are important. They pass around the nest in the air as scents or through touch, and alter the behaviour of the group. For example, among leaf-cutter ants, if there are not enough food-gatherers, the level of the 'food-collecting' pheromone drops, and this makes some worker ants take up that task which, in turn, makes more of the pheromone.

▶▶ **Read further › chemicals**
pg13 (b33)

▸ The first ants to detect a leaf source lay an invisible pheromone trail for the others to follow.

In big mammals that form societies, such as elephants and killer whales, a female – the matriarch – is in charge

◀ *A wolf shows its superiority among the pack by bearing its teeth. The junior or submissive wolf crouches with his head and tail down.*

Order in the group

Animal societies have many ways of organizing their hierarchy so that members of a group learn who is the dominant animal. Grooming is very important among such animals as dogs and apes. This is not only for cleanliness – senior members are groomed by more junior members. The terms 'pecking order' and 'top dog' come from this process among birds and dogs, such as wolves.

Read further › wild dogs
pg13 (e22)

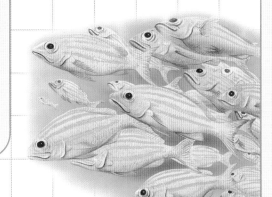

Safety in numbers

Some fish pack so closely in a shoal, that they are almost touching. The whole group twist and turn as one glinting, whirling mass. This confusing, fast-changing sight makes it very difficult for a predator to pick out and attack a single individual. Birds form dense flocks for the same reason.

◀ *When swimming in a shoal, fish coordinate their movements with their neighbours. When the fish are all together, but each acting independently, the group is known as an aggregate.*

Read further › predators
pg13 (o30)

CREATURE COMFORTS

• Only two kinds of cat are social. The lion forms prides of up to ten members. Cheetahs form 'coalitions' of two to four males – often brothers – that hunt together for many years.

• Most wild dogs are social. South American bush dogs form packs of about ten, which hunt together to catch prey bigger than themselves.

▼ *Chimpanzees often live in large groups of up to 100 members. Smaller sub-groups form within the main troop, but members come and go often in these. This is called a 'fission-fusion' society.*

One of the gang

Most kinds of monkeys and apes live in societies where many pairs of eyes and ears are alert to danger so that one can warn the rest. They gather in troops to distract or frighten an enemy. They spread out to feed, and if one finds plenty, the others share it. Adults without offspring may even assist parents by 'babysitting'.

Read further › parental care
pg30 (q2)

 Check it out!

• http://www.nwtwildlife.rwed.gov.nt.ca/
  NWTwildlife/wolf/behaviour.htm
• http://www.careforthewild.org/chimps.asp

In insect societies such as those of bees and ants, a female – the queen – is in charge

a b c d e f g h i j k l m n o p q r s t u v w

Hibernation and migration

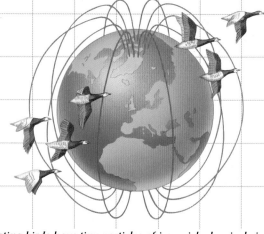

▲ *Migrating birds have tiny particles of iron-rich chemicals in their brains, which may detect the Earth's natural magnetic field.*

I N THOSE regions of the world where the seasons are distinct, there are warm, bright summers when food is plentiful, followed by cold, dark winters when living conditions are very difficult. Small creatures such as insects can survive the long winter as hard-cased eggs, but mammals and birds cannot. They use two main methods or survival strategies: 'stay or go'. One is to stay in the region but go into a very deep sleep, known as hibernation, then wake up the next spring. The other is to migrate – travel away on a long journey – returning the following spring.

Flying visits

Birds are the main migrants. They can travel long distances quickly. Many types of geese and ducks live in Europe, Asia and North America during winter. Then they fly north in the spring to the Arctic, where the brief summer encourages an 'explosion' of plants, insects and other foods. The birds nest and raise their young in the Arctic, then fly back again in autumn.

▶▶ Read further > flying / nesting
pg10 (f2); pg22 (r3)

CREATURE COMFORTS

• Some animals such as lemmings and locusts migrate only occasionally. After several years of good conditions in their home region their numbers increase too much. They run out of food so set off looking for new places to live.

• Some animals actually migrate up and down mountains. Mountain sheep and cattle climb to high pastures in summer and descend to sheltered valleys in winter.

Learning the way

Each spring, reindeer, known as caribou in North America, trek northwards to the treeless Arctic tundra, where mosses, grasses and other plants grow in the long hours of summer sun. Youngsters learn details of the route each year, and use their experience as they grow older to guide the next generation.

▶▶ Read further > seasonal changes
pg15 (b32)

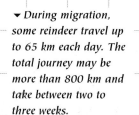

▼ *During migration, some reindeer travel up to 65 km each day. The total journey may be more than 800 km and take between two to three weeks.*

The greatest mammal migrant is the Pacific grey whale, which travels 20,000 km annually

▶ *Some salmon are born in freshwater streams, stay for a year or two, then migrate out to sea. Years later, they migrate back to the same stream they were born in, to lay their own eggs and then die.*

Finding the way

Animals such as whales and birds combine methods of navigating – using the position of the Sun, Moon and stars, large landmarks such as mountains or cliffs, and even the Earth's magnetic field. In water, migrating salmon and other fish, turtles and lobsters 'smell' and 'taste' amounts of natural chemicals that change in different rivers or parts of the ocean.

▶▶ Read further › whales
pg35 (b22)

'Knowing' the way

Monarchs are the champion insect migrants. Each spring these butterflies leave a few over-wintering areas of southwest and North America and fly north, feeding and breeding as they go. Their offspring return in autumn. They do not live long enough to learn the route – instead it is in-built, or instinctive.

▶▶ Read further › breeding
pg30 (d2)

▲ *Monarch butterflies can fly up to 80 km each day.*

▼ *Badgers live and hibernate in 'setts' that have many different entrances and tunnels. In mild weather they may wake up from their hibernation and wander outside for a drink and to eat.*

IT'S A FACT

• The furthest travelling migrant is the Arctic tern that flies from the Arctic to Antarctica and back each year – covering 35,000 km.

• The birch mouse hibernates up to eight months a year, spending over two-thirds of its life asleep.

Cold and slow

Only warm-blooded animals truly hibernate. (Winter inactivity of cold-blooded animals is called torpor.) Most are rodents and bats, but badgers and hedgehogs also hibernate. They feed hungrily in autumn to build up stores of fat, then fall into a deep winter sleep. Body temperature drops from about 40°C to as low as 3°C. Breathing is very slow and the heart beats once every few minutes.

▶▶ Read further › storing food for winter
pg15 (b32)

Check it out!
• http://www.enchantedlearning. com/coloring/Hibernate.shtml

A bear's temperature during its winter sleep drops only 5°C, so this is not true hibernation

Camouflage and mimicry

▲ *Chameleons change colour (camouflage) to communicate and control their temperature (going darker makes them warmer).*

A RAINFOREST OR coral reef may seem empty of creatures – until a closer look reveals 'leaves' that are really butterflies (*see pg25 [d37]*), or 'seaweed' that is a fish. Blending with the background is called camouflage. It keeps animals hidden from predators – and also helps predators hide from their prey before catching it. Camouflage usually involves colours, patterns and shapes, but it can also include movements, sounds and smells. Other animals have bright colours and patterns that act as a warning that they are venomous or have poisonous flesh. When one animal copies another, but is itself harmless, it is called mimicry.

● Master of disguise

The chameleon – a type of lizard – can change its colour and pattern in minutes to blend in with its background. It uses tiny coloured particles, called pigments, in its skin that can clump together so they are not seen, or spread out to show their hue. For example, when the chameleon moves from a leafy branch to dry twigs, it changes from green to brown.

►► **Read further › stick insect**
pg31 (b30)

IT'S A FACT

• Batesian mimicry is when several harmful, poisonous or horrible-tasting animals all resemble each other.

• Mullerian mimicry is when a harmless animal avoids being eaten by copying a harmful one.

● Keeping still

►► **Read further › spitting spiders**
pg13 (b33)

Movement is an important part of camouflage. A crab spider or flower mantis must keep perfectly still, hidden among the same coloured petals. The slightest movement would reveal it not only to its prey – it may itself become prey for a watching lizard or bird.

◄ *Crab spiders are so-called because they can walk sideways (like crabs). Some can even change colour to match different flowers.*

Not all camouflage is visual – some animals roll in dung to disguise their scents

Flat as a 'carpet'

The carpet shark – or wobbegong – spends most of its time simply lying on the seabed. Its body is flattened and has lumps and frills in shades of yellow, green and brown, which resemble the seaweed-covered rocks. As an unsuspecting fish swims up to it, the carpet shark lurches forwards and opens its huge mouth to swallow the victim in one gulp.

▾ *Wobbegongs remain close to the shore in shallow water, sometimes partly lying in the open air when the tide falls.*

Model and mimic

The animal that a mimic copies is called the model. The venomous coral snake is a model for mimics such as the non-venomous king snake or the milksnake. Bigger predators that try to eat a coral snake get bitten, suffer pain, and learn to avoid it and any animal that looks like it. This is how mimics gain protection from predators.

▴ *Milksnakes are mostly nocturnal snakes that feed on amphibians and small rodents. The order of the colours in their pattern differs slightly from their model, the coral snake, but is close enough to fool any potential predators.*

▸▸ **Read further › cobra**
pg20 (i12)

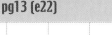

▸▸ **Read further › anglerfish**
pg13 (e22)

Spots and stripes

▸▸ **Read further › leopard**
pg12 (n2)

In the forest, light shines through leaves and creates many patches of brightness and shade thus creating patchy camouflage. Most forest cats, from margays to leopards *(see pg12 [r10])* have spotted coats, as do young deer and baby wild boar, which lie silent and still in the undergrowth while their mothers feed. Animals that live in cold regions are pure or patchy white to blend in with the shade and light of the snow and ice.

CREATURE COMFORTS

• Many fish are darker on their upper side and lighter on their underside for camouflage in sunlit waters where light comes from above. This is called countershading.

• The mimic octopus can change its colours and move its tentacles to pretend to be a ray, an anglerfish or even a shark, warning off predators.

◂ *The Arctic hare of Canada and Greenland has a thick, almost pure white coat to keep warm and blend in with the snow. But its coat may moult to a thinner, grey-brown one for the summer.*

◂ *Snow leopards have thicker, lighter coats than other leopards, to blend in with their icy mountain habitat.*

Check it out!
• http://www.howstuffworks.com/animal-camouflage.htm

The hognosed snake rolls over and plays dead, and even smells dead, to deter predators

a b c d e f g h i j k l m n o p q r s t u v w

Courtship and territories

COURTSHIP IS an essential part of male and female animals getting together to mate (breed). Courtship can involve sight, sound, smell, movement or all of these. Courting partners check they are both of the same species, fully-grown and able to breed and are strong and healthy. This gives their offspring the greatest chance of being strong, fit and healthy. In some animals, breeding also depends on owning a territory. This is an area that the animal occupies and defends against others. Usually it is the male partner that performs the main courtship display and holds the territory.

Breeding requirements

Male antelopes, such as topi, gather in a traditional area and snort, prance and clash to see who is the biggest and strongest. The winners take charge of small territories, called 'leks', at the centre of the area, where they are more attractive to females. A lek-less male cannot breed. Birds such as grouse also use the lek system.

▲ A grouse struts around with his head pointed upwards, whilst fanning his feathers and making bubbling and scraping noises to attract a female.

Partners for life

Many animals mate with different partners each year, either one or several. However, some larger birds, such as swans, are monogamous – they mate for life. This means they only have one partner throughout their lifetime. A female swan lays up to eight eggs, which she cares for until they hatch, then both parents look after them.

▶▶ **Read further › breeding**
pg30 (d2)

▼ Each spring pairs of swans renew their relationship by twining their necks together and calling to each other.

Male elephant seals are so huge, and battle so fiercely, they may crush their own mates and offspring

1   2   3   4   5   6   7   8   9   10   11   12   13   14   15   16   17   18   19

▼ *Frigatebirds live on uninhabited islands of the Tropical Pacific, Atlantic and Indian Oceans. They can form colonies of thousands of pairs during breeding time.*

Putting on a show

Many male birds, such as frigatebirds, put on amazing courtship displays as they puff out their bright red throat pouch to attract a mate. Peacocks fan their feathers, sing loudly and flap or jump. Birds have good colour vision, so brightly coloured plumage (feathers) is important during courtship rituals. The male robin's red breast becomes brighter during breeding time to attract a female.

▶▶ **Read further › nests** pg22 [r3]

▶ *The call of the red howler monkey of South America can carry more than 5 km.*

Morning chorus

Each dawn the forest fills with loud howls, squawks and songs. Mammals and birds are announcing to others nearby that they are well and healthy and occupying their territories. If a howler monkey does not howl one morning, rivals know the territory is vacant and soon try to take over.

▶▶ **Read further › apes** pg23 [p22]

▲ *A peacock is chosen by a female (peahen) according to how magnificent his brightly-coloured tail feathers are and how proudly he displays them.*

CREATURE COMFORTS

• A home range is where an animal roams and feeds. It may mark the area with scent, but unlike a territory it is not defended by chasing out others.

• A male Bengal tiger's home range is often more than 100 sq km; a female's is up to 25 sq km.

▼ *Rutting between male mammals such as wild goats determines who gets to mate; the loser will have to wait for the chance to compete with another male.*

Fight to the death?

Male mammals such as sheep, goats, cattle and deer *(see pg19 [i26])* show their strength and fitness by rutting – battling with rivals. The contests look fierce, but there is usually a set of natural 'rules' to avoid serious injury.

▶▶ **Read further › antelope and deer** pg19 [b22]

🔘 **Check it out!**

• http://ladywildlife.com/animal/ birdcourtship.html

The male crab spider spins a small web over the female to avoid being eaten by her, as they mate

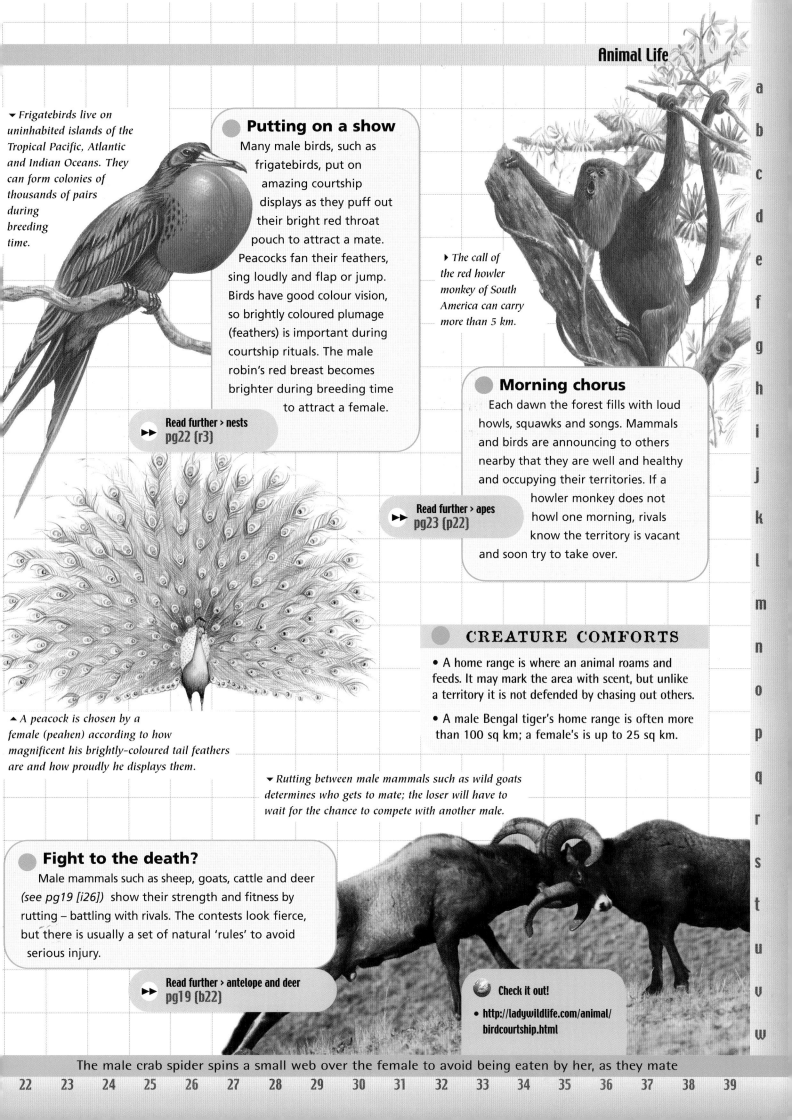

Breeding

BREEDING OR reproduction – making more of the same kind – is essential for all living things. Animals use many different methods. Some small and simple creatures, such as tiny tree-shaped hydras in ponds, simply grow offspring as 'stalks' on their own bodies. This is asexual (one-parent) reproduction. But most animals reproduce sexually, when a male and female mate. The male's sperm join with – fertilize – the female's eggs. The majority of creatures, from worms to birds, lay eggs. Only mammals and a few reptiles, fish and invertebrates, give birth to babies.

Wrong offspring

Read further › nesting pg22 (r3)

The cuckoo is a 'reproductive parasite'. The female cuckoo replaces an egg in another bird's nest with her own egg, then flies away. The host bird looks after the new egg and chick, which pushes out the other chicks after it hatches.

▲ These flycatchers are the host parents of this cuckoo chick, which may eventually grow bigger than they are.

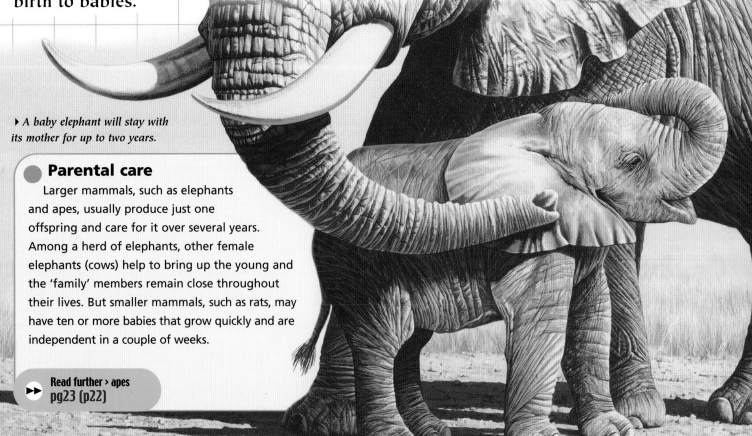

▸ A baby elephant will stay with its mother for up to two years.

Parental care

Larger mammals, such as elephants and apes, usually produce just one offspring and care for it over several years. Among a herd of elephants, other female elephants (cows) help to bring up the young and the 'family' members remain close throughout their lives. But smaller mammals, such as rats, may have ten or more babies that grow quickly and are independent in a couple of weeks.

Read further › apes pg23 (p22)

The ostrich lays the world's biggest egg, 16 cm long and 14 cm deep

Fatherly duties

Most animals develop inside their mother, growing as eggs before being born to continue growing physically independent of the mother. However, seahorses, though they begin life in their mother, actually develop from eggs inside their father. The female seahorse lays her eggs in a pocket-like pouch on the male's front. The eggs hatch two to six weeks later into young seahorses. Then the father seems to 'give birth' as the small babies pop out of his pouch.

Read further › sea creatures
pg13 (j22)

▶ *The seahorse anchors itself to eel grass using its tail, which is specially adapted for grasping.*

No male needed

Some aphids (greenfly), flatworms, leeches and other smaller animals reproduce by parthenogenesis – the female can produce eggs or babies without having mated with a male. Usually the stick insect lays eggs by parthenogenesis whereby the offspring will grow into females. But if she has mated with a male, the eggs will hatch into both females and males. Parthenogenesis also occurs in some fish, stick insects and in types of whiptail and wall lizards.

▲ *Stick insects often have leaf-like bodies as a camouflage (they adopt the colour of the background) to avoid danger.*

Read further › camouflage
pg26 (f12)

▼ *The chance of fertilization among frogs is increased by the male releasing his sperm straight onto the jelly-covered eggs that the female lays in the water.*

Outside the body

On land, a female and male animal usually mate when the sperm pass into the female's body to fertilize the eggs – internal fertilization. However, in water, many kinds of frogs, fish, shellfish, worms and other animals simply release their eggs and sperm into the water, and leave fertilization to chance – external fertilization.

To scale

Each square = 4 cm across
Different sizes of birds' eggs

Ostrich egg 16 cm long
Hummingbird egg 1 cm long

LONGEST GESTATION

Animal	Length of gestation
Elephant	600–660 days
Whale	520 days
Rhinoceros	490 days
Walrus	480 days
Giraffe	460 days

Check it out!
• http://www.saburchill.com/chapters/chap0031.html

Ostriches are unusual because several females lay eggs in one nest, then the male cares for the chicks

22 23 24 25 26 27 28 29 30 31 32 33 34 35 36 37 38 39

Animals in danger

I N THE next few hours, somewhere in the world, a species of animal will become extinct – completely disappear and be gone for ever. This will probably be because of human activity, such as cutting down a rainforest to turn it into farmland or polluting water with chemical pesticides. The species may be a rare kind of bird or mammal, but it is more likely to be a small insect such as a bug or beetle. Indeed, it is likely that the species is not even known to science, because only about 1.8 million animal species have been described and named by scientists. The real number of species living in the world today could be more than 20 million.

CREATURE COMFORTS

• Nearly half of the world's tropical rainforests have been destroyed over the last 50 years to clear the way for farmland or buildings.

• In some regions, powdered rhino horn or crushed tiger bones are worth more than gold for the medicinal qualities they are believed to possess.

IT'S A FACT

• It is estimated that one-quarter of all bird species are under some type of threat to their survival, mainly from habitat disturbance.

• Today's 'hot spots' of risk include the rainforests of Central and South America, West Africa and Southeast Asia, and coral reefs across the tropics.

Precious but passing away

The biggest threat to animals is the destruction of their habitat. For example, this occurs when a forest is cut down for timber and the trees are not replaced, or when houses, factories and roads are built through the countryside. When an animal such as a golden lion tamarin's natural habitat disappears, it has nowhere to breed or find food, so it may decline in numbers until it eventually dies out altogether.

▶ *Golden lion tamarins are victims of habitat destruction in coastal rainforests in Brazil. However, many have been bred in captivity, and released back into the wild.*

▶▶ **Read further › habitats**
pg34 (d2); pg35 (r32)

 Check it out!

• http://worldkids.net/eac/facts. html

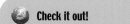
All five kinds of rhinos are under threat, largely from poachers who kill them for their horns

▸ *The pet trade is responsible for many thousands of parrot captures each year. Some species of parrot have already become extinct due to capture and habitat destruction.*

Varied threats

The rare river dolphins of the Amazon, Ganges and other great waterways face many problems. Their survival is threatened by water pollution from chemicals that are pumped into the river from factories and dams that block their way. They must compete with fishermen for food supplies and avoid boats with slashing propellers that may harm them and noisy engines that disrupt their sound-sonar communication system. Outbreaks of disease and being hunted for their meat are also great threats to their survival.

▶▶ **Read further › dolphins**
pg11 (s22)

▲ *The number of Ganges river dolphin are now fewer than 1000.*

Rare meat

As people in poor countries struggle to feed themselves, some turn to hunting wild animals for meat or to sell as pets at large markets in towns. This fast-growing trade affects apes *(see pg23 [q34])*, monkeys, wild pigs, antelopes, bats, tropical birds such as parrots, lizards and snakes, especially in poor countries such as some parts of Africa.

▶▶ **Read further › pet and meat trade**
pg34 (p9)

Hunting and collecting

Tigers are often killed for their luxurious fur, their teeth, which are used in unconventional medicines, and by people who enjoy the 'thrill' of hunting dangerous animals. Great white sharks are caught so often, both for 'sport' and because they may menace swimmers, that they have become a threatened species.

▶▶ **Read further › hunted animals**
pg35 (b22)

▼ *The biggest type of tiger, the Siberian tiger, is very rare, with fewer than 200 surviving in the wild.*

Pollution

Power stations and vehicles send fumes up into the air, factory pipes pour poisons into the rivers, lakes and seas, and pesticide and herbicide chemicals are washed down from farms. These damaging chemicals, along with disasters such as oil spills, pollute vast areas of sea and coastline and can kill fish and clog up birds' wings so that they are unable to fly and hunt.

◂ *Oil spills devastate coastal wildlife, killing fish and sea creatures that cannot breathe in the contaminated water and so suffocate.*

▶▶ **Read further › fish defence**
pg23 (d34)

The Javan rhino is perhaps the most threatened of all mammals – fewer than 100 are alive today

a
b
c
d
e
f
g
h
i
j
k
l
m
n
o
p
q
r
s
t
u
v
w

Conservation

THE GIANT panda, mountain gorilla, Siberian tiger (*see pg33 [o23]*) and Californian condor are some of the best-known animals under threat. But there are many thousands more, in almost every habitat around the world. Conservation does not mean simply saving a few species in zoos or small parks. Whole habitats and ecosystems – communities of living things in their natural surroundings, from mountains and deserts, to woods, swamps, and even deep oceans – are set aside as nature reserves and sanctuaries. Conservationists protect species and their habitats so that creatures and plants can survive together in a natural way.

▲ *Today, there are more than 170 Californian condors – 50 of which fly free in the wild.*

● Captive breeding

Well-run zoos and wildlife parks are extremely valuable for conservation. Rare animals such as Californian condors can be studied there to save them from extinction. The last pair of Californian condors living in the wild were captured to be bred. By 1998, there were 150 birds, 35 of which were released into the wild. This number continues to increase. Captive breeding allows animals to reproduce and then be prepared for gradual release back into suitable habitats in the wild.

▶▶ **Read further › birds of prey**
pg13 [e22]; pg18 [j12]

◀ *Gorillas face threats from forest clearance and illegal hunting.*

● Animal army

Some creatures need protection from humans – poachers and hunters who kill them for meat or for valuable parts such as ivory tusks, fur or gorilla hands. Rangers and guards help to prevent this, but they cannot protect every animal. Animals would be safer if the pet trade was banned and governments ensured that people had enough food so they could stop hunting endangered animals for meat.

▶▶ **Read further › hunting**
pg33 [d22; k22]

▲ *Giant pandas have inefficient digestive systems and to sustain their huge body weight – usually more than 100 kg – they have to spend more time eating than most other animals.*

Slow to recover

In 1966 the mass hunting of some great whales was banned. By 1986 all species of great whales were protected. But these animals breed very slowly, producing a new calf only every two or three years. Blue whales number about 15,000 around the world, with about 200 births annually. It will take many more years for them to reach safe numbers again.

Read further › dolphins
pg11 (s22); pg33 (d22)

▲ *Commercial hunting of whales was banned in 1986, but many smaller whales are often caught in fishing nets, causing them to drown, or are harpooned during illegal hunting.*

CREATURE COMFORTS

• Great efforts have been made in China to save the 1000 or so remaining giant pandas, by setting aside reserves where they can live in peace and safety.

• Some reserves are linked by 'breeding corridors' to enable pandas to mate away from their area. This helps to solve the problem of inbreeding – breeding within families – where animals in an area become too closely related and thus weaker.

▼ *Eco-tourism enables people safely to view animals such as elephants in their natural habitat and generates funds for conservation projects.*

Check it out!

• http://www.kakaporecovery.org.nz/kids/index.html

IT'S A FACT

• The first new large mammal to be discovered in 50 years is the sao-lao. Like an antelope, it was found in the 1990s in Vietnam.

• Since 1960, one new species of monkey has been found in the Amazon rainforest in Brazil almost every year.

Read further › parrots
pg33 (d32)

Animals versus animals

The kakapo is a rare, flightless parrot from New Zealand. There are fewer than 100 kakapos surviving in the wild. One of the birds' major threats is from animals such as rats and foxes, which eat kakapo eggs and chicks, introduced by people into the bird's natural habitat. To save the species, conservationists have bred the kakapo in captivity before moving them to islands without these predators.

▸ *The kakapo is one of the world's most endangered parrots.*

Animal value

Some people in the world are extremely poor, while others are very wealthy. Eco-tourism can help conservation by sharing out the wealth. People pay to see rare animals in their natural habitats through such activities as going on safari. The money raised through these activities provides the funds for new wildlife sanctuaries and conservation projects.

Read further › elephants
pg30 (q2)

Global warming may harm wildlife such as penguins, who live on the ice caps, which are gradually melting

Glossary

Alveoli Tiny air spaces or bubbles inside the lungs, where oxygen is taken into the blood from breathed-in air.

Aquatic An aquatic animal lives in water.

Asexual reproduction When a living thing produces offspring without a mate.

Brachiation Hanging while swinging with a pendulum-like motion, as when gibbons swing through tree branches.

Browser An animal that eats mainly leaves from taller plants such as trees and bushes.

Cache A hidden store of, for example, food.

Camouflage When an animal is shaped, coloured or patterned to merge or blend in with its surroundings.

Canines Long, sharp teeth near the front of the mouth used to stab and rip at prey.

Carnivore An animal that eats mainly meat, usually by catching other animals.

Circulatory system Parts of an animal – usually the heart, blood vessels (tubes) and blood – that spread nutrients around the body, and collect wastes and leftovers for removal.

Conservation Saving or preserving animals and their natural surroundings or habitats.

Detritivore An animal that eats rotting bits of once-living things, such as the meat off an old carcass, or tiny edible particles in mud.

Digestive system Parts of an animal that take in food and break it into tiny pieces, small enough to be taken into the body.

Echolocation Method used by animals such as bats to find their way and locate objects in darkness, by sending out pulses of very high-pitched sounds and listening to the echoes.

Endoskeleton A skeleton inside the body, consisting of strong supporting parts, usually bones, to hold the body together.

Extinct When a particular species of living thing has died out and disappeared for ever.

Flukes The two broad parts or lobes of the tail of a whale, dolphin or porpoise.

Gills Body parts to help breathe underwater. They are usually feathery or frilly and take in the oxygen, which is dissolved in water.

Grazer An animal that eats mainly grasses and other ground or low-growing plants.

Habitat A particular type of surroundings or living place with its own kinds of animals and plants, such as a pine wood, grassland, desert, lake, sandy seashore or deep sea bed.

Hibernation When an animal's body temperature falls, usually to less than 10°C, and the animal falls into a deep sleep, usually to survive the long, cold season.

Home range An area where an animal usually roams and feeds, but which it does not defend, unlike a territory.

Incisors Teeth at the front of the mouth, usually shaped like chisels, with sharp straight edges for gnawing and nibbling.

Invertebrate An animal that does not have a backbone (vertebral column).

Krill Shrimp-like animals that thrive in vast shoals (groups) in the ocean and are food for larger animals, such as penguins, seals and whales.

Lateral line Line of tiny sensors along a fish's body, to detect movement in the water.

Migration Long-distance journeys, usually carried out at certain seasons, there and back again each year.

Mimicry When one animal looks like another (the model) to gain an advantage, for example pretending to be a poisonous animal when it is not itself poisonous.

Model In animal mimicry, the creature that the mimic looks like or pretends to be.

Muscle Part inside an animal's body that gets shorter, or contracts, to move the body.

Parthenogenesis When a female animal is able to produce offspring without a mate.

Pheromone A chemical substance produced by an animal, which affects the actions and behaviour of others of its kind.

Plankton Tiny plants and animals that drift in the water of seas, oceans and large lakes.

Predator An animal that hunts and catches other creatures, called prey, for its food.

Prey A creature that is hunted or caught as food by another animal, called the predator.

Respiratory system Parts of an animal that take in oxygen from the air.

Sexual reproduction When a living thing produces offspring with a mate.

Social Social animals usually live with others of their kind, and communicate with them by sight, sound, smell and touch.

Tentacle An arm- or leg-like body part that is bendy all the way along, without joints.

Terrestrial An animal that lives on land.

Territory An area or place where an animal lives and feeds, and which it defends by chasing away others of its kind.

Thrust The force pushing an animal forwards, as from the legs of a land creature.

Torpor When a cold-blooded animal's body becomes so cool that the animal can no longer move about.

Vertebrate An animal that has a backbone (vertebral column), usually as part of its inner skeleton of bones.

Warning colours Usually bright colours and patterns to warn other creatures that an animal is harmful, such as being poisonous.

Index

Entries in bold refer to main subjects; entries in italics refer to illustrations.

A

air
  breathing **16–17**
  flying in 10
albatrosses 10
algae 15, *15*
alligators 12
amphibians
  breathing 17, *17*
  muscles 9
anglerfish 13, 27
animal societies **22–23**
anteaters 13
antelopes
  hunting 33
  movement 8
  speed 9
  territories 28
ants 13, 22, *22*, 23
apes
  breeding 30
  hunting 33
  social groups 22, 23, *23*
aphids 15, 31
Arctic hare 27, *27*
axolotl 17, *17*

B

babies **30–31**
backbones 8
badgers 25, *25*
barn owl 18, *18*
barracuda 19, *19*
batesian mimicry 26
bats
  echolocation 18, *18*
  extinction 33
  flying 10, 11
  hibernation 25, *25*
  meat eaters 12
beaks 12, 14
bears
  hibernation 25
  muscles 9, *9*
  teeth 12, *12*
beavers 14, 20
bees 21, 22, 23
beetles 14, 32
birds
  breathing 16, 17
  communication 20, 29
  courtship **28–29**
  digestive system 16, *16*
  extinction 32, 33

birds (*continued*)
  flying 10
  hunting 12, 13
  migration 24, 25
  muscles 9
  reproduction 30
  societies 22, *22*, 23
birds of prey 12, 13
black rhino 14
blue whale 10, *10*, 13, 35, *35*
bluefin tuna 11, *11*
body language 20
bones 8, 9
brain 16, 24
breathing **16–17**, 25
breeding **30–31**
  captive breeding 34
  communication 20, 21
  courtship **28–29**
  inbreeding 35
browsers 14
bugs
  extinction 32
  movement 8
  plant eaters 14, 15
burrowing animals 9
butterflies
  camouflage 26
  migration 25
  warning colours 21

C

Californian condor 34, *34*
camouflage 9, **26–27**
canine teeth 12, *12*, 15
captive breeding 34
caribou 24, *24*
carnassial teeth 12, *12*
carnivores **12–13**, *12*, 14
carpet shark 27, *27*
caterpillars 14, 21
catfish 19, *19*
cats
  eyes 18
  meat eaters 12, 13
  social groups 23
  warning signals 20
cattle, wild 14, 24, 29
centipedes 12
chameleons 26, *26*
cheetahs 8, *8*, 9, 23
chemicals, pheromones 22
chimpanzees 21, 23, *23*
claws 12
cloaca 16, *16*
cobras 20, *20*
cold-blooded animals 13, 17, 25

colour
  camouflage 26
  feathers 29
  warning signals 21, 26
colugo 11
communication **20–21**, 29
condors 34
conservation **34–35**
copepods 15
coral snake 27
countershading 27
courtship **28–29**
crab spider 26, *26*, 29
crabs 17
crocodiles 11, 13, *13*
cuckoo 30, *30*
cuttlefish 20

D

deer
  camouflage 27
  food 14
  rutting 29
  sense of smell 19, *19*
defences 8, 19, 23, 26, 27
diatoms 15, *15*
digestion **16–17**
digestive system 16, *16*
dogs *see* wild dogs
dolphins 11, *11*, 33
ducks 24

E

eagles 12, 13, *13*, 18
ears 18, 19
eating
  digestion 16
  meat eaters **12–13**
  plant eaters **14–15**
echolocation 18, *18*
eco-tourism 35, *35*
eggs **30–31**, *31*
elephant seal 28
elephants
  babies 30, *30*
  food 14
  hearing 19
  social groups 22
endangered animals **32–33**
endoskeleton 9
excretory system 16
exoskeleton 9
extinction **32–33**
eyes 18, 19

F

falcons 10
feathers, colour 29

fertilization, eggs 30, 31
fighting 29
fin whale 10, *10*
fins 10, 11
fish
  animal societies 22, 23
  breathing 17
  camouflage 26, 27
  lateral line sense 19
  migration 25
  muscles 9, 10
  reproduction 30, 31
  senses 19
  shoals 23, *23*
  swimming 10, 11, 23, *23*
  warning colours 21
flatworms 17, *17*, 31
flippers 10, 11
flower mantis 26
flukes 11
flycatchers 30, *30*
flying **10–11**
flying lemur 11
flying squirrel 11, *11*
food
  digestion 16
  meat eaters **12–13**
  plant eaters **14–15**
forest cats 27
forests 9, 26, 32, 35
foxes 21, 35
frigatebirds 29, *29*
frogs
  breathing 17, *17*
  breeding 20, 31
  communication 20
  food 12
  movement 11, *11*
  reproduction 31, *31*
  warning colours 21

G

Ganges river dolphin 33, *33*
gazelles 8, 14
geese 24
giant panda 34, *34*, 35
gibbons 9
gills 17, *17*
giraffes 14, *14*
gizzard 16
gliding animals 10, 11, *11*
goats, wild 29, *29*
golden eagle 13, *13*
golden lion tamarin 32, *32*
gorillas 34, *34*
grazers 14
great white shark 33
greenfly 31

The publishers would like to thank the
following artists who have contributed to this book:
Syd Brak, John Butler, Jim Channell, Richard Draper, Chris Forsey, Luigi Galante, Ian Jackson,
Emma Louise Jones, Doreen McGuiness, Andrea Morandi, Terry Riley, Steve Roberts
Sarah Smith, Rudi Vizi, Christian Webb

The publishers wish to thank the following sources for the photographs used in this book:
p35 (c/r) Barry Harcourt/AFP, p35 (b/l) PICTOR/AFP

All other photographs are from:
Corel, digitalSTOCK, John Foxx, MKP Archives, PhotoDisc